Tom Hanks Biogra...
An Extraor
Beyond the S

Note:

....
....
....
....
....
....
....
....
....

By Rogelio Olea

Copyright © 2023 by Rogelio Olea
All rights reserved.

The content of this book may not be reproduced, duplicated, or transmitted without the author's or publisher's express written permission. Under no circumstances will the publisher or author be held liable or legally responsible for any damages, reparation, or monetary loss caused by the information contained in this book, whether directly or indirectly.

Legal Notice:

This publication is copyrighted. It is strictly for personal use only. You may not change, distribute, sell, use, quote, or paraphrase any part of this book without the author's or publisher's permission.

Disclaimer Notice:

Please keep in mind that the information in this document is only for educational and entertainment purposes. Every effort has been made to present accurate, up-to-date, reliable, and comprehensive information. There are no express or implied warranties. Readers understand that the author is not providing legal, financial, medical, or professional advice. This book's content was compiled from a variety of sources. Please seek the advice of a licensed professional before attempting any of the techniques described in this book. By reading this document, the reader agrees that the author is not liable for any direct or indirect losses incurred as a result of using the information contained within this document, including, but not limited to, errors, omissions, or inaccuracies.

TABLE OF CONTENTS

Introduction

Chapter 1
Hollywood's Famous Everyman

Chapter 2
Always on the Move

Chapter 3
Building a Reputation and Career

Chapter 4
Splashing into Success

Chapter 5
Hitting the Big Time

Chapter 6
Life Is Like a Box of Chocolates

Chapter 7
Living at the Top

INTRODUCTION

Tom Hanks may not be as attractive as Tom Cruise or Will Smith, but he is just as successful, with 7 consecutive blockbusters grossing more than $100 million. Tom Hanks was born Thomas Jeffrey Hanks on July 9, 1956 in Concord, California. Janet Marylyn, a hospital worker, and itinerant chef Amos Mefford Hanks had their third child. Tom's family had been seriously fragmented since he was a child, and he divorced in 1960. Tom had to shift from one area to another after his parents divorced. Tom moved ten times when he was ten years old. Tom's adolescence was ruined by his traveling lifestyle. Tom didn't cause any problems, but he was so strange and introverted that no one recognized him. However, there is always a tremendous fire waiting to ignite in Tom. Then he discovered the area where he wanted to shine - the stage. Tom Hank studied theater at California State Chabot College for two years before transferring to the University of California. Tom spends a lot of time going to the movies by himself at the moment. He didn't date anyone; he simply drove to the theater, purchased a ticket, saw the play, and became utterly engaged in it.

Tom met Vincent Dowling, the head of theater at Cleveland, Ohio, during his years in drama. He became an intern here on the suggestion of this individual. After finishing high school, Tom worked for three years, gaining invaluable knowledge in all aspects of stage management, from lighting to design. For his performance in Shakespeare's The Two Gentlemen of Verona, Tom received a little Cleveland award for Best Actor in 1978. This is one of the few occasions when he plays a villain. Tom married his first wife, Samantha Lewes, the same year. They have a son and a daughter. However, it appears that Tom Hanks has realized that the stage is not for him. He moved to New York in 1979 and made his cinematic debut in the low-budget horror picture He Knows You're Alone. Tom's acting career began well, despite the fact that he was only cast in minor roles. The next year, he was cast as the lead in the ABC television series Bosom Buddies. The film was well received by critics, but due to poor ratings, it was only aired for two seasons. In any case, the Bosom Buddies remain a significant milestone in

Tom's life. This is the film that introduced him to his second wife, actress Rita Wilson. When Rita was cast as a supporting character in the film, they met. They married the following year after Tom divorced his first wife in 1987, have two children, and live happily ever after.

Tom was fortunate to win the lead part in Splash in 1984. This $8 million film unexpectedly grossed $69 million at the box office and garnered an Oscar nomination. After years of hard work, Tom eventually found success with the fantasy comedy Big in 1988. The amusing and emotional story of a youngster who turned an adult overnight earned Tom a Golden Globe and an Academy Award nomination for Best Actor. the most effective. Tom Hanks' name is now legally recognized in Hollywood. A few years later, Tom was still receiving pictures on a regular basis, but his career had stagnated. Fortunately, he rose to prominence again in 1992 with a role in the psychological comedy A League Of Their Own. When compared to the beginning of his career, this is the point at which Tom's acting abilities have significantly developed and reached their height. With the good film Sleepless in Seattle, Tom Hanks' career entered its golden age. The story of a widower who discovers new love through radio waves has become a romance genre classic. The "chemistry" between Tom Hanks and Meg Ryan was so outstanding that they went on to star in You've Got Mail, which was likewise a huge success. Tom's performance was described as "charming" by Time magazine, and most critics saw him as a prominent star of the romantic comedy genre. That same year, Tom Hanks surprised viewers once more as a gay lawyer with AIDS suing a firm in Philadelphia for discrimination. Tom shed over 16 kg and shaved his head to look the part. One of Tom Hanks' best acting talents is his willingness to make sacrifices for the sake of art. In order to play Chuck Noland, a guy abandoned on a desert island in Cast Away in 2000, he had to shed up to 25kg. People had to praise Tom Hank for his "Oscar-worthy" performance in Philadelphia. This is an excellent observation, considering it was this Andrew Beckett character that earned Tom his first Oscar for Best Actor in 1993. This is a gift to compensate for the loss. In 1988, he lost his role in Big to Rain Man's Dustin Hoffman.

Following Philadelphia, Tom Hanks captured the globe in 1994 with his portrayal in the legendary picture Forrest Gump, which broke the law in theaters and grossed over $600 million worldwide. This part also helped Tom get another best actor nomination. Forrest Gump remains one of Tom's iconic characters "for a lifetime" in his acting career. Tom Hanks' next role is as astronaut Jim Lovell in Apollo 13, directed by Ron Howard and starring Kevin Bacon and Bill Paxton. The picture gained critical acclaim and nine Academy Award nominations that year. Throughout his career, Tom Hanks has worked extensively with the renowned director Steven Spielberg. The films directed by the talented director and starring one of the world's most talented actors, such as Catch Me If You Can (2002), which received two Oscar nominations, Bridge of Spies, which received six nominations, and Saving Private Ryan, which won five Oscars. Tom Hanks is one of the top names Hollywood producers want to uncover, having achieved success in both art and commercial films, with both potential and guaranteed money. Tom Hanks continued to pursue his interests outside of performing in the years that followed. He is a prominent director, producer, and screenwriter. Tom Hanks and Steven Spielberg collaborated on the HBO miniseries The Pacific in 2010. This picture is honored to have been nominated for a Golden Globe.

CHAPTER 1
HOLLYWOOD'S FAMOUS EVERYMAN

Tom Hanks earned consecutive Best Actor Academy Awards for his outstanding performances in Philadelphia (1993) and Forrest Gump (1994), two very different films. This had not occurred in Hollywood since the 1930s, when actor Spencer Tracy received the same honor. Hanks has retained his elevated entertainment-industry position in the decade following these notable victories. The seasoned actor is one of Hollywood's most powerful figures, earning $20 million each feature picture.

Tom Hanks is regarded as Hollywood's everyman, which means that he excels at playing everyday characters to whom almost everyone can relate—and he does so powerfully. Many film critics have linked Hanks to two prominent stars of Hollywood's Golden Age, Jimmy Stewart and Cary Grant, when he first rose to popularity in the mid-1980s. Hanks, like the lanky Stewart, excels at playing the man next door, the type of charming individual you immediately trust and want to get to know as a friend. And, like the smart Grant, Hanks can be clever, glib, and charming on screen. Premiere magazine noted in a discussion of the top movie performers of the last 15 years, "You begin to get an idea of Tom Hanks's singular and irreplaceable role in the history of popular movies when you imagine subtracting him from that history."

Steven Spielberg presented Tom Hanks with the American Museum of the Moving Image's coveted Lifetime Achievement award in April 1999. "Tom is from that old-time America, when tradition and pride in your country were things you didn't scoff at," the acclaimed filmmaker remarked of his actor buddy and frequent coworker. On another occasion, Forrest Gump producer Steve Tisch said of Hanks, "The man is as nice, as honest, as professional, as personal, as he seems to be."

Not Just "Mr. Nice Guy"

Although the humble Hanks is sometimes referred to as "Mr. Nice Guy," he dislikes the moniker. "I'm probably as nice as the next guy, but you know, I have my moments," Hanks says. It can be aggravating when people have that expectation." Sally Field, who co-starred with Hanks in Punchline (1988) and Forrest Gump, feels that Hanks has more layers than his pleasant image suggests. "Yes, he's very entertaining, funny, and easy to get along with." "But you know there's someone else underneath, someone dark," Field says. "There is a sad, gloomy side. That's what makes him so appealing on TV."

Much of Hanks' "dark' ' side derives from his odd background, when his parents divorced and remarried other partners on a regular basis. Over the course of five years, Hanks had two different stepmothers, several step siblings, and moved multiple times. As a result, he was always the new kid on the block. Despite how traumatic that may seem, Hanks, who is highly reclusive and avoids open talks of personal problems, openly dismisses his rough childhood. "We were just a completely normal broken family." "Everyone was married and lived in different places, and nobody gave it much thought," he adds.

Hanks never imagined himself as an actor as a child. His main interests were sports and, in particular, the United States space program. He aspired to be an astronaut one day. (Hanks was able to realize this vision while playing astronaut Jim Lovell in the 1995 film Apollo 13.) Hanks became interested in the theater and make-believe during high school. When he fell under the lure of the acting industry, it became the only option for this extremely inventive youth with a self-deprecating—and goofy—sense of humor. Years later, long after he had perfected his creative trade, Hanks would remain boyishly excited about his career choices. "I have this insane job where they pay me ludicrous amounts of money to put on other people's clothes and pretend to be someone else for a while."

CHAPTER 2
ALWAYS ON THE MOVE

Thomas Jeffrey Hanks, a distant cousin of President Abraham Lincoln, was born on July 9, 1956, in Concord, California, a town about 23 miles northeast of San Francisco. Tom Hanks was the third of four children born to Amos and Janet Hanks. His mother worked as a waiter. His father (nicknamed "Bud" by friends) was a restaurant cook who previously wanted to be a writer and had always wanted to move to Australia. Those dreams were dashed when Amos married Janet and the couple became parents. Amos Hanks and his family relocated frequently when he changed occupations in the food sector when he was caught up in the obligations of a large household. Janet, on the other hand, stayed at home to care for their children.

Amos and Janet, who had been married for ten years, became parents for the fourth time in 1961, with the birth of their son James. Domestic emotional and financial stresses had already severely harmed the couple's relationship. Amos vanished one day in January 1962, without telling his children where he was going. He went home a month later after visiting Reno, Nevada, where he filed for divorce from Janet. That night, he urged his three oldest children (Sandra, Lawrence, and Tom) to pack a few of their belongings—there was only enough room for them to carry one or two favorite toys—and hurry out to the pickup vehicle in the driveway. (Jimmy, who was still a newborn at the time, stayed behind with Janet Hanks.) Amos drove his three kids to Reno, where he'd already found a new employment as a hotel/casino chef and rented a small basement apartment. Amos enrolled Tom in Reno's Holy Child Day Care Center because, unlike the older children, Tom was too young to be left alone while Amos worked.

There were soon new adjustments in the disjointed Hanks family. Amos married his landlady, Winifred Finley, on April 23, 1962, four days after his divorce from Janet was finalized. She was recently divorced and had five children of her own. Tom and his siblings had gained a new family. Their father, who was never adept at communicating, didn't explain the current development. Overnight,

Tom and the seven other children were sharing a small house's tight basement rooms, while the newlyweds lived above. Years later, Hanks reflected on the perplexing set, saying, "I remember in school we had to draw a picture of our house and family and I ran out of places to put people." I threw them up on the roof. I drew dad resting in bed because he worked so hard in the restaurant."

After a while, the family relocated to a larger home in Sacramento, California, and subsequently to Pleasant Hills, California. Tom was the most adaptable of Amos' three children to the ever-changing domestic situation. The five-year-old child, as the new Mrs. Hanks remarked, "could roll with the punches." "You could get lost in the shuffle or you could be a loudmouth," Tom later said of being the youngest member of his crammed household. "I went with the latter option."

Amos and Winifred divorced after only two and a half years of marriage. Amos had his three children pack their possessions and drive off during the night, this time to Oakland, across the bay from San Francisco, without providing any meaningful explanation. This change was especially upsetting for Tom, who was suddenly more mature and observant. His coping method was to relegate his second family to the past. Hanks told Us magazine in 1984, "I wouldn't remember their names if they showed their faces today."

The Hanks family lived in San Mateo, California, for a while with Amos's sister Mary, who was a dedicated member of the rigorous religious organization known as the Nazarenes. Following their unstructured childhood, the befuddled youngsters struggled to obey the rules and order in their aunt's household. "We weren't allowed to watch the Three Stooges; there were an awful lot of rules... awfully long prayers," Tom explained. On rare weekends and usually for all major holidays, Tom and his brothers were bused to their mother's home in Red Bluff, upstate California. Tom rarely visited his younger brother Jimmy, who stayed with his mother, because these encounters were uncommon. As a result, the two lads were complete strangers to one another. It wasn't until the late 1980s that they became friendly. By then, Jimmy had followed Tom's lead and become an actor as well.

After a few months, the Hanks left Mary's house and moved to a series of small, low-rent apartments, many of which were in Oakland. Because Amos Hanks worked long hours at his restaurant, the three kids were mostly on their own. This unstructured pattern suited Tom, who enjoyed the company of his siblings and sister. "The coolest place to be was at home, because we were always cracking each other up," he would later say, despite his lonely upbringing. "Goodness surrounded me."

When talking about his eccentric childhood, Tom mentioned, "We did our own laundry." We were meant to keep the house clean, but it was never.... We were fully unsupervised, but we got into a lot of trouble." Tom enjoyed spending hours in front of the television, lost himself in series like Star Trek and news coverage of America's space endeavors. Another favorite activity for the Hanks family was when Amos would throw a mattress in the back of his truck and take the family to a local drive-in theater, where the father and children would watch movies while relaxing in the truck bed.

As the youngest of Amos' three children, Tom was expected to do less around the house. "Because I had less at stake," he explains, "I developed an observational point of view." This behavioral attitude persisted throughout adulthood, with Tom preferring to be the bystander in social situations.

A SUDDEN CHANGE

Amos Hanks was studying culinary and hotel management at a local vocational college in 1966. He had lately met Frances Wong, a waitress and divorced mother of three daughters. They quickly fell in love and married. France's youngest child joined the new family while her two older daughters went to live with their father. Contrary to Amos' expectations, the latest upheaval in their lives swiftly disillusioned them. Frances was incredibly structured and attempted to adapt her stepchildren to her strict ways. It caused domestic upheaval. Sandra quickly left, preferring to live with her mother. Tom and his older brother Larry established headquarters in the basement of their new home, only interacting with the others during mealtimes. Larry afterwards relocated to Red Bluff to be near his mother and sister.

Tom had a mother, two stepmothers, and had lived in ten different residences in five different cities by the age of ten. As a result of all these travels, he had learnt how to rapidly adapt to new schools and peers. Despite his introverted temperament, he developed the external personality of a class clown. However, Tom was savvy enough not to cross the line with his teachers: "If the teacher wasn't laughing, I'd shut up," he once stated.

Tom went to Bret Harte Junior High in Oakland a few years later. He had gained the ability to mix with a number of social groupings at school at this point. However, beneath his clown face, he was insecure. He saw himself as an outcast who had been abandoned much too frequently. Even as an adolescent, he spent a lot of time watching TV, especially anything related to outer space. Tom was so pleased when Stanley Kubrick's film 2001: A Space Odyssey was released in 1968 that he saw it 22 times in local theaters.

Hanks joined the First Covenant Church, an Oakland-based Fundamentalist Christian congregation, when he was 14 years old. It offered him a much-needed sense of belonging and acceptance. He thrived on the group's social features, but after a few years he left, explaining, "When you're young and idealistic, you tend to view things in absolute terms, and the absolutes didn't pan out, even within the confines of that place."

OPENING NEW VISTAS

Hanks remained a mediocre student at Oakland's Skyline High School. He continued to thrive as a class clown with a keen sense of humorous timing, and he participated in a few sports, including soccer and track. (As he grew closer to his full height of 6 feet, 1 inch, his track teammates dubbed him "Lanky Hanks.") When school wasn't in session, he worked as a soda vendor at Oakland A's baseball games for a spell. Despite having a girlfriend in high school, the future actor subsequently admitted that he was not popular with the opposite sex: "I was a little too geeky, a little too gangly, and much too manic."

Tom decided to explore theater after seeing a friend's performance in a high school play. At Skyline High, he enrolled in Rawley Farnsworth's drama class, eventually taking six courses with his new instructor. Hanks assisted Farnsworth as stage manager for a school production of the musical My Fair Lady. Later, Tom played the bus driver in the school's production of Tennessee Williams' Night of the Iguana.

Farnsworth was among the first to notice Hanks' unusual magnetism onstage, describing him as someone "you can't take your eyes off and you want to see everything they do." Following that, Tom was cast in the humorous role of Sir Andrew Aguecheck in Shakespeare's Twelfth Night. Hanks learnt from Farnsworth that a novice needs to try a range of parts in order to become a successful performer. Then, no matter how successful he becomes, he should always seek out new acting opportunities. These were important lessons for Tom to remember, especially as his cinematic acting career took off in the 1980s.

Hanks played a prominent role in the Rodgers and Hammerstein musical South Pacific during his final year at Skyline. Tom got the school's equivalent of an Academy Award for his stirring portrayal as Luther Billis. In later years, Hanks would constantly praise Farnsworth, as well as fellow classmate John Gilkerson, for their early encouragement of his acting goals. In fact, when Hanks accepted his Academy Award for his performance in Philadelphia in 1994, he recognized these two guys as his inspirations for his award-winning performance in that picture.

Tom attempted to build a stage character for himself in the early stages of his acting career. On play programs during his senior year, for example, Hanks spelt his first name "Thom." He quickly realized that the name change was pretentious and returned to the original spelling.

Tom was living apart from his family by his final year at Skyline, boarding with a single mother (who he knew from his church group) and her three children. To supplement his income, Hanks worked as a bellman at the Oakland Hilton Hotel on weekends and during the summer. Tom loved his job, especially when he got to transport cinema legend Sidney Poitier to the airport in the hotel limousine or carry bags for celebrities like Cher and tennis champ Billie Jean King. Some of these frequently humorous celebrity interactions would emerge as anecdotes when Hanks rose to renown as a movie actor in the 1980s, making the rounds of late-night TV talk shows.

ON TO COLLEGE

Because Tom Hanks had just a C average in high school, his possibilities for college admission were limited. Only Chabot Community College, located in nearby Hayward, accepted him out of the three colleges to which he applied. Hanks has yet to decide on a career path. He claimed he was "waiting for something to conk me on the head and say, 'This is the direction you want to go in.'" Hanks was back at home with his father and stepmother.

Hanks initially did not engage in campus theatrical productions at Chabot, but he frequently traveled to San Francisco or Berkeley to see plays produced. One day, he ran into his high school classmate John Gilkerson, who was also a Chabot student and persuaded Hanks to return to the theater. This nudge encouraged Hanks to audition for a school production of Thornton Wilder's Our Town, in which he earned a leading role and received rave reviews.

Enrolling in Herb Kennedy's Drama in Performance course at Chabot was a watershed moment for Hanks. Students were forced to read numerous plays and then attend a local production of each. One of Hanks' most formative experiences was reading Eugene O'Neill's The Iceman Cometh and then seeing it played live at the Berkeley Repertory Theater. "I came out of the theater enthralled by what those people had done that night," Hanks later remembered. That was something I'd never seen before." Hanks shared his incredible experience with his teacher, and Kennedy guided the student into further dramatic discoveries. Hanks did not forget Kennedy's advice after achieving success. Years later, in the summer of 1981, when Hanks costarred in the TV series Bosom Buddies, Kennedy enticed him back to Chabot to star in a campus production of the play Charley's Aunt.

Hanks spent much of his time at Chabot doing theater craft classes and working backstage for college shows. He found great delight in his carpentry talents and his ability to use whatever materials he could find and turn them into stage productions.

Hanks received a scholarship in theater craft in 1976, allowing him to transfer to California State University, Sacramento. The school had a tiny theatrical department, but it allowed for a lot of student participation. Initially, Hanks intended to work backstage as a stage manager, lighting designer, or set builder. He knew he liked being near the theater. It gave him a strong sense of belonging. Another of Hanks' qualities was his uncontrollable clown instinct. Whatever the situation, he was always making amusing remarks or performing ridiculous stunts.

A BREAKTHROUGH

Susan Dillingham, who went by the stage name Samantha Lewes, was one of Hanks' theater arts classmates. They were inseparable. A romantic relationship immediately formed and blossomed into love. Meanwhile, Hanks' enthusiasm for performing in front of the audience, rather than behind it, resurfaced. (As Hanks put it, "I soon discovered that the most magical place to be was on stage.") When some of his friends were cast in a campus production but he was not, Hanks took charge. He tried out for an upcoming performance of Anton Chekhov's The Cherry Orchard at the Sacramento Civic Theater. He was pleasantly delighted to be cast as the servant Yasha, for which he earned positive feedback.

The Cherry Orchard's out-of-town director, Vincent Dowling, was pleased by Hanks' emerging talents. Dowling was the artistic director of the Great Lakes Shakespeare Festival in Cleveland at the time. He invited Hanks and a few others to work as summer interns there.

When the school year concluded, Hanks, Lewes, and other college pals eagerly made their way east.

The interns were not compensated for their labor as backstage workers painting sets, hanging lighting, and so on. However, if they also had theater roles, their pay was low. This spurred Hanks to audition for tiny parts, which began to come his way soon after. Just getting paid to act was a "phenomenon" for Hanks. This was huge in my opinion." When he wasn't in a play and had any downtime, Hanks enjoyed going to Cleveland Indians baseball games, even if the professional team was struggling. Years later, interviewers would take his ardent support for the poor local ballplayers as another proof of Hanks' everyman qualities. Hanks stated that he was "perfectly happy with their position at the bottom of the [American League] standing."

When Hanks and Samantha returned to Sacramento that fall, he decided not to attend college. Samantha was expecting a child, and he needed to provide for his girlfriend and their child. He went to work as an assistant stage manager at the local Civic Theater for $800 a month. Colin, the couple's son, was born on November 24, 1977.

In the summer of 1978, Hanks and Samantha came to Ohio with their baby for another season at the Shakespeare Festival. Hanks was now landing greater playing roles with the ensemble, whose plays frequently toured the area. In Two Gentlemen of Verona, he played Proteus, and in The Taming of the Shrew, he played Grumio. The Cleveland Critics Circle awarded Hanks Best Actor of the Year for his spectacular performances that season.
When the Great Lakes Shakespeare Festival's 1978 season ended, Hanks and Samantha made a big decision. Beyond Cleveland and Sacramento, they needed to broaden their professional horizons. They elected to live in New York City rather than try their luck in Los Angeles, the Hollywood capital, where they thought they would be lost. Friends persuaded Hanks that he could at least gain employment with the Riverside Shakespeare Company while waiting for his Broadway break there. Hanks and Lewes sold his well-traveled Volkswagen Beetle to fund the perilous relocation because

they were down to their last $35. The $850 from the sale of the car was used to start a new life in New York, where they hoped to gain fame and wealth.

CHAPTER 3
BUILDING A REPUTATION AND CAREER

Tom and Samantha Hanks and their infant son Colin moved into a walkup apartment on West 45th Street in the fall of 1978, in a decaying Manhattan area known as Hell's Kitchen. Initially, the only furnishings in their cockroach-infested apartment were a few milk crates. The family survived on the weekly unemployment payments Hanks received following his recent stint at the Great Lakes Shakespeare Festival, as they had few savings left after the move from Cleveland. When the family's finances were tight, they joyfully took a few bucks from Hanks's sister Sandra, who scraped together money by collecting and redeeming old soda bottles.

Hanks began his acting career with the Riverside Shakespeare Company, where he appeared in a production of Machiavelli's Mandrake. It was a worthwhile experience, but Hanks earned little or no compensation for his services. He auditioned for TV advertisements and daytime soap operas, as do most new actors. However, he was unsuccessful in these tryouts.

Hanks and Samantha struggled to adjust to life in New York. They had to care for their infant in addition to competing for possible employment assignments in the show business sector. Meanwhile, Hanks went through a crash school on putting up a resume, having head photos taken by a photographer, practicing audition sequences, and so on, in order to go on casting rounds.

Hanks soon matured as a result of his daily struggles in New York. "I had an ongoing responsibility that a lot of actors can shirk," Hanks explained. "We lived on the edge, but thank God, no one got sick." At the same time, Hanks lobbied for a break in his chosen field. The actor has never forgotten those trying times. "Every now and then, I'd take a hundred dollars and drive from city to city looking for work." I took jobs that no one else wanted. I'd wake up at night, go into the bathroom, stare in the mirror, and wonder, 'What happened to me? 'My career has ended before it has even begun.'"

RETURNING TO AN OLD HAUNT

With no lucrative work available in Manhattan, Hanks and his family returned to the Great Lakes Shakespeare Festival for the summer 1979 season. During his stay, he appeared in A Midsummer Night's Dream and a musical called Do Me a Favor. His part in the latter production, which was about Shakespearean actors touring across greater Dublin, required him to appear as a boy playing a girl who, in turn, is playing a boy. Festival director Vincent Dowling described his protégé as "the best Shakespearean clown I ever knew, because he was seriously real and seriously funny at the same time."

When Hanks returned to Manhattan that fall, he was pleasantly surprised to receive a feature-film job. Simon Maslow, Hanks' new personal manager, arranged the gig. Maslow had sought talent representation for the young actor with the J. Michael Bloom business, which had offices in both New York and Los Angeles. The Bloom Agency cast Hanks in the 1980 film He Knows You're Alone. It was a low-budget slasher film that was to be shot entirely on Staten Island. For a seasoned Shakespearean actor, the task may have appeared to be a professional step down. Hanks, on the other hand, was ecstatic at the prospect of making his film debut and earning $800 for a little part. He later remarked, "It was the first job I had wearing regular pants, you know, as opposed to [medieval] sword belts, leather jerkins [a close-fitting, sleeveless coat], and sandals."

The film is about a murderer with a knife who massacres numerous women in a bridal party. Hanks plays Elliott, a psychology student who tries to explain to a cast member (and the audience) what drives the lunatic to go on murdering sprees.

Hanks worked three days on the quickie film, which resulted in seven minutes of screen time for him. "I didn't know what I was doing," he acknowledges of his film debut. I just walked there and learnt how to hit a mark [a point indicated on the set floor by chalk marks or bits of masking tape to establish an actor's position for the impending camera shot]." Hanks' character appears in the jumbled plot, talks about the killer's psychological makeup, and then vanishes from the story. Years later, Hanks lamented, "I don't even get killed [in the story]."

He Knows You're Alone was published without fanfare in September 1980. The entry was described by Tom Buckley of the New York Times as "the latest in a ghoul's parade of cheaply made horror movies." "That people should pay money to see such films is ridiculous when you think about it," wrote a Los Angeles Times critic. He Knows You're Alone was a box office flop. Years later, it would resurface in VHS format for the home entertainment industry.

CALIFORNIA BOUND

Hanks and Samantha decided to formalize their relationship now that his career was on the rise. They married on January 4, 1980, at the Church of the Holy Apostles in New York City. During the ceremony, their small son, Colin, raced around the church.

Meanwhile, Hanks had a major studio feature-film credit to his acting record. Hanks' representation began pitching the role to casting directors, which resulted in job auditions in New York. This, in turn, piqued the curiosity of West Coast casting agents. Before long, Hanks, 23, was pulling together cash to fly to Los Angeles, where his agent had scheduled tryouts for him.

Hanks arrived at his reps' West Coast office wearing a sweat suit, bright-eyed and still innocent. His frustrated agent promptly handed him a few hundred dollars to purchase more acceptable attire for important casting rounds. Hanks had a significant appointment at ABC-TV, where the network sponsored a talent program aimed at uncovering new faces for the company's upcoming shows.

When Hanks arrived for his meeting with Joyce Selznick and Jan McCormack, who ran ABC's talent development program at the time, he already had a propensity for outstanding auditions. Hanks had acquired a protective feeling of apathy about these casting sessions after being rejected at so many previous tryouts. This can be a positive attitude for actors because it allows them to be relaxed and spontaneous in such situations. To better prepare for such situations, Hanks reminded himself that he was "just as good as 50% of the competition." And I thought I was better than 45% of the competition. So if the remaining 5%, who are gifted geniuses I will never be able to touch in a million years, don't show up for an audition, I've got a chance. "I might get lucky."

Jan McCormack remembered meeting Hanks for his ABC tryout years later. "When Tom walked in, there was a couch in the room. And he flipped over it, like if he'd tripped. And all you said was, 'Wow.' So we had him read for a comic part. Then we questioned him whether he was serious. And he simply jumped right in. That was a young Jack Lemmon [a well-known, Oscar-winning actor]."

Because of the fantastic impression he made on return visits to ABC, Hanks was signed to a $50,000 contract that gave the network a year to cast him in one of their TV shows. This "holding" deal permitted Hanks' agency to pursue other types of projects, such as feature films, made-for-TV movies, and TV specials. ABC auditioned Hanks for several of its series in the hopes of immediately utilizing its new employee. As a result, Hanks was cast in an episode of the long-running television series The Love Boat. Hanks appeared on an episode of "Friends and Lovers" that aired on October 25, 1980. Watching Hanks' small-screen debut would be a rewarding event for him and his family.

Meanwhile, he received a phone call from ABC officials about one of their new TV shows for the 1980 fall season. The half-hour show was called Bosom Buddies, and Hanks was in talks to portray one of the stars. He was astounded by the turn of events, given that he had not even auditioned for the project. In retrospect, the celebrity would add, "I had no idea what I was getting myself into." I would have probably choked if someone had told me."

ACTING IN A DRESS

Edward K. Milkis, Thomas L. Miller, William Boyett, and Chris Thompson, seasoned executive producers, packaged Bosom Buddies.

They had worked on popular TV sitcoms including Laverne & Shirley. The new offering was a comedy based on the traditional act of two males dressed as women. This trick, for example, was successfully exploited in the 1959 film Some Like It Hot.

The plot of Bosom Buddies revolves around two young New York ad agency hotshots who share an apartment. When their dilapidated building is demolished and they are looking for new digs, one of their coworkers offers they move into her building. The only issue is that it is an all-female community. Nonetheless, inspired by the low rent and the prospect of being around gorgeous, young ladies, the two guys carry out their mad idea. They dress as ladies and pretend to be their own sisters in order to be admitted to the Susan B. Anthony Hotel for Women.

ABC had first targeted two other performers for the sitcom, but when those efforts failed, the producers went to Peter Scolari and Tom Hanks. Scolari, 26, was a character in the recently canceled ABC comedy Goodtime Girls. On Bosom Buddies, he was cast as Henry Desmond, a junior copywriter with aspirations of becoming a novelist. Hanks auditioned and was cast as Kip Wilson, a struggling illustrator who aspires to be a painter, at the last minute. Paramount TV picked up the pilot for distribution after it was shot.

Bosom Buddies was slated to show on Thursday nights, sandwiched between two of ABC's long-running comedies, Mork & Mindy and Barney Miller. As a result, when Bosom Buddies began on November 27, 1980, many of the viewers who turned in for those popular shows stayed on that channel to see it. The new entry received favorable home viewer ratings, ensuring its continuation throughout the season. The unoriginal premise did not sit well with the trade publication Variety. It did, however, give the program a qualified thumbs up, stating, "The key to this kind of humor is the flair of the performers—and Peter Scolari and Tom Hanks get a good chemistry going between them, buttressed by fine timing for young players."

With an experience primarily in Shakespearean theater work, Hanks was initially hesitant to take on a TV project. Hanks, like Scolari, was nervous about being in feminine disguise each week, especially because, even with full makeup, he appeared too masculine to be a credible lady. The co-stars quickly learned that their makeovers for each new episode were a time-consuming task that would soon outlast its welcome with the public. Nonetheless, they gave the show their all.

"Everyone was trying to prove himself," Hanks said of Bosom Buddies. It took a season for it to be enjoyable, for me to grasp that it was, at its foundation, the same process as creating theater.... There was a lot of anxiety." During his on-the-job training, Hanks discovered that giving a television performance differs from doing theatrical work. "The camera does a lot of the work for you," he discovered. That you don't have to yell as much.... You don't even have to be energetic.... I learned to pay attention to people's subtle cues to stop talking."

Costarring in Bosom Buddies honed Hanks' acting abilities in various areas. "It accelerated us. The whole business was about doing your best to provide the goods. If you couldn't deliver them well, you had to deliver them poorly as long as they were delivered. It's a case of flying by the seat of your trousers. You ask as many questions as you can, but it inevitably comes down to 'Never mind, just do it.' You cannot be sluggish. It took over our entire lives.... It was a busy, busy time."

Hanks and Peter became fast friends on Bosom Buddies during their first season as they plowed their way through the often-trite weekly plots; they frequently ad-libbed to give the program more spark, zip, and uniqueness. Because Hanks and his family had relocated to the San Fernando Valley outside of Los Angeles, the two twenty something actors commuted to work together every day. On the way to the TV soundstage, Hanks and Peter practiced their on-camera antics.

By the time Bosom Buddies finished its first season in the spring of 1981, the network had given the show the green light (an industry phrase for approval) for a second season the following fall. Hanks was earning $9,000 each episode at the time, which enabled him to repay the money he borrowed when he initially went to Los Angeles.

When the series returned in October 1981, ABC reduced the then-tiresome female drag routine and gave Hanks and Scolari more opportunities to appear as quick-witted, imaginative gentlemen on the chase for beautiful women. Unfortunately, the network lost faith in the series, as seen by the show's broadcast time being constantly switched on the program schedule. Even die-hard fans of Bosom Buddies were irritated by the inability to predict when the comedy will air.

After 38 episodes, ABC canceled the Bosom Buddies series in the spring of 1982. Hanks, like the rest of the cast, was relieved to see the show come to a close. They were all fatigued from the hectic production schedule and thought the comedy's premise had worn thin. Samantha gave birth to Hanks' second child, Elizabeth, on May 17, 1982, just as they were escaping the weekly grind.

SEEKING NEW CAREER HORIZONS

Hanks' ABC contract called for him to participate in episodes of the network's other ongoing TV shows. He appeared on Taxi in the spring of 1982 and on Happy Days the following fall. In the latter, he played the Fonz's (Henry Winkler's) wimp-turned-karate-expert classmate. Hanks also appeared in two episodes of the comedy Family Ties. He was cast as Meredith Baxter-Birney's character's drunken younger sibling.

In a more significant professional move, Hanks landed the lead role in Rona Jaffe's two-hour TV film "Mazes and Monsters." The telefilm was shot in Canada and was based on Jaffe's best-selling 1981 novel. It portrayed Hanks as a college student who grew so engrossed in a role-playing game (based on Dungeons & Dragons) that he literally lost himself in it, attempting to outwit adversaries and overcome complicated barriers. The film and novel were inspired by a true story.

Hanks based his characterisation on personal experience, as he would with many subsequent acting roles. "I had a perception of the game that people who hadn't played it wouldn't have," he explained. It can be rather frightening if you have an especially vivid imagination. The deeper, darker demons that we all harbor within us can truly come to the fore." This was a difficult acting assignment for Hanks. "When the cameras roll, I have to let Tom Hanks fade into the background." But it is the most enjoyable aspect about it. I feel like I'm working at a lot higher intensity than I have in the past."

On December 28, 1982, Rona Jaffe's "Mazes and Monsters" premiered on CBS and got decent numbers. According to the New York Times, "the younger actors [in the cast] are required to carry the film, and they do so with remarkable skill." Hanks' performance was praised by Variety as a "solid turn."

FACING AN UNCERTAIN FUTURE

Actors, like other artists, can never count on a steady career and salary. Hanks was now on his own after being a television series co-star, hustling for guest appearances on other people's shows. His doubts surfaced once more, and he began to doubt his future in show business. Growing conflicts in Hanks' household added to his professional problems. Samantha, now a mother of two, was angry that her career ambitions as an actress and producer were being repressed and sacrificed for Hanks'. The couple's squabbles became more intense. Falling back on childhood patterns, Hanks did the same with his rocky marriage as he had done with his terrible family life. He discovered that burying oneself in work was the best solution to his issues. The issue was that acting gigs were still few and, in his opinion, too far apart. Then a screenplay about a mermaid entered his life and forever altered his career.

CHAPTER 4
SPLASHING INTO SUCCESS

By the time Tom Hanks appeared in a Happy Days episode in 1982, Ron Howard, who played Richie Cunningham, had departed the long-running TV program to pursue a career in film filmmaking. Howard, on the other hand, continued to watch the weekly sitcom and was impressed by Hanks' guest appearance. In addition, he continued to play on the Happy Days baseball club, where he met Hanks, who came in for a few games. Howard could tell Hanks had a wealth of potential that was just waiting to be discovered.

After directing the humorous picture Night Shift (1982), Howard was working on a new screen project, Splash (1984), with his producing partner Brian Grazer. Already, the film has encountered problems. It was originally scheduled for a United Artists release, but that was canceled due to reports that another studio was developing a similar-themed movie (which never materialized). Later, Splash piqued the interest of Disney executives, who thought the love tale of a mermaid and a young man would make a good debut entry for Touchstone Pictures, Disney's newly formed division dedicated to producing pictures for older audiences. Splash was given a $8 million budget by Disney.

Because of the prospect of a film actors' strike, the Splash crew was pressed to complete casting and begin filming before the planned walkout. Comedian John Candy, an SCTV star, was being considered for one of the film's two starring male characters, who are brothers. The directors, however, were having difficulty finding the perfect actor to play the second sibling. Dudley Moore, Chevy Chase, Bill Murray, and John Travolta, to name a few, were either unavailable or declined the role. The Splash team eventually went to the current crop of TV names for potential candidates. During the process, Howard remembered Hanks and invited him to audition. "He read, and he was fantastic," Howard said. We simply stopped looking."

During the audition process, the directors recognized that Hanks, who was originally cast as the rude Freddie, had the dramatic range and warmth to play Allen Bauer's brother. Allen is an idealistic hero who struggles to commit to a romantic relationship. In the film, he re-encounters a mermaid he first met as a child. Allen understands that his long-held affection for this odd creature has kept him from falling in love with anyone else.

Candy was cast as the womanizing Freddie after Hanks was cast in a pivotal role. Daryl Hannah, a lovely blond actress who was somewhat unknown at the time, was picked as the mermaid. Before production began, Hanks, Daryl, and the crew went through extensive underwater training. "I was a certified diver" after 16 days of training, according to Hanks. There was no danger at all. We weren't diving in deeper than 40 feet of water. In truth, it was enjoyable—at least for me. I'm sure Daryl didn't enjoy it. She was wearing that fin!"

WORKING IN THE DEEP

The underwater preparation was for the film's aquatic scenes, which were shot in both the Bahamas and in studio tanks. Hanks and Hannah had to operate underwater without oxygen tanks for those sequences. During the laborious process, they filmed an underwater clip before swiping to a nearby lifeline to take breaths of air. Because it was impossible to talk, let alone be heard, underwater, the performers and technicians devised a system of hand signals to communicate with one another.

Hanks acquired some helpful acting lessons for the scenes on dry land, which helped him change his humorous acting style. Developing this kind of variety is really beneficial to an actor. "Your job is not to go toe-to-toe with John Candy and get laughs," Howard warned Hanks. If you do that, this film will be a flop. All you have to do is adore the girl. Just look at her and fall in love." "If we don't believe this girl is magic to you," the filmmaker continued, "we don't have a movie." Hanks' attitude about his cinematic character changed once he adjusted to the expectations. "I was never saying, 'Let's do this because it'll be funny,'" Hanks explains. "I was saying, 'Let's do this because it'll be fun.'" It would help to round out the guy." Hanks learnt to tone down his performance for Splash in comparison to his unsubtle humorous acting on Bosom Buddies. He had to let the humor come from his reactions rather than broad physical actions. Throughout the production, Hanks demonstrated a remarkable sense of improvisation, which impressed Ron Howard.

Making Splash, more importantly, taught Hanks humility and responsibility. At one point, Hanks failed to pay attention to the daily call sheet, which specified the shot schedule for the following day. As a result, Hanks arrived on set one morning less prepared than he should have been. "There was a scene with a huge plot point and a huge character point that caught me off guard," Hanks recalls. We did it over and over again. We eventually got it.... Ron remained composed. "However, he summed up the entire experience by saying, 'It would have been nice if you were a little more prepared today.'" It was a lesson Hanks would never forget. Hanks used his professional blunder to develop a strong working and personal relationship with Howard. Splash helped Hanks in various areas besides helping him grow as an actor: It sparked his interest in scuba diving, and his film earnings enabled him to purchase a reflector telescope to develop his interest in astronomy and outer space.

Splash was an instant hit when it was released in March 1984. The critics were equally enthused. According to Variety, "Hanks makes a fine leap from sitcom land." David Denby of New York magazine was particularly enthusiastic about Hanks' cinematic potential, calling him an accomplished comic who is "good-looking and relaxed enough to be a leading man." "He commands the emotional center of the scenes," Denby continues, "holding your sympathy in place." Splash grossed over $69 million in domestic distribution. "That's a lot of money, and you can't get much better right out of the box," Hanks exclaimed. It's ideal."

INVITATION TO A BACHELOR PARTY

While Splash was in post production in late 1983, no one expected it to be a smash hit, Hanks signed on for the picture Bachelor Party (1984). It was a vulgar film comedy about a wild night for a befuddled young school-bus driver who was about to marry. The comedy had already begun filming at Twentieth Century-Fox when the producers realized that Paul Reiser and Kelly McGillis were miscast in the lead roles. Hanks and Tawny Kitaen were hired as replacements in a last-minute scramble. Wendie Jo Sperber, a Bachelor Party cast member who was a regular on Bosom Buddies, recommended Hanks for the role.

Hanks was initially skeptical of this project, wondering "what the challenge was going to be." He played a more active role in bringing the story to life this time, with the consent of director Neal Israel and the producers. In the process, he worked to tone down some of the cruder portions of the R-rated film. "I wasn't interested in throwing myself at a wall or dropping my pants," he reasoned. "We needed something better." Aside from the $60,000 price, what drew him to the project was a certain topic in the film. "I thought it said something about fidelity in life today," Hanks commented.
Bachelor Party was released three months after Splash in June 1984. Much of the plot's ridiculous humor was overcome by the excellent performers. Variety praised Hanks in his nice-guy role for his "overabundance of energy." Despite her complaints about this lowbrow film, New York Times critic Janet Maslin noted, "Mr. Hanks's suave smart-alecky manner owes a lot to [TV and screen comedian] Bill Murray, but he's funny and engaging even if he isn't doing anything new." Bachelor Party was a summer blockbuster, collecting $38.4 million in domestic distribution.

THE WORKAHOLIC YOUNG STAR

With two box-office triumphs under his belt, Hanks was quickly becoming a household name in Hollywood. He grew increasingly popular in the media. For example, the press questioned why he had appeared in a lowbrow picture like Bachelor Party. "I'm an actor," he replied. An actor must perform. What else should I do but sit around the house?"

In fact, under normal circumstances, Hanks preferred to do just that. "I just like to piddle around," he admitted on one occasion. I mostly talk on the phone, watch television, and read. I enjoy boredom; I keep the interesting stuff for work." However, the ongoing feud between Hanks and his wife, which he kept hidden from the public eye, colored his time at home, impairing his potential enjoyment of being a family man with two children. It drove Hanks to accept any decent filming assignment, particularly those that brought him on location and away from his wife, with whom he shared so few interests.

In this state of mind, Hanks rushed to Washington, D.C., to star in The Man with One Red Shoe (1985). The spy spoof was a reworking of an older French film that was popular throughout Europe. Hanks spent several hours learning the mechanics of playing the violin for his role as a concert violinist caught up in CIA activities. He was determined that his fingering and bowing would appear natural on camera, despite the fact that the actual sounds of his violin were dubbed by a professional musician. Despite the efforts of Hanks and co-stars Jim Belushi and Carrie Fisher, this film parody was a flop. In retrospect, Hanks considers this to be his weakest film.

Without taking a break, Hanks began work on Volunteers (1985), which was shot in Mexico. This comedy from 1962 reunited him with John Candy. Hanks plays Lawrence Bourne III, a snooty Yale graduate with an unhealthy gambling addiction, in Volunteers. Lawrence takes on the role of a Peace Corps volunteer headed to Thailand to avoid angry creditors. As a part of the US government's goodwill mission, he is saddled with a group of idealistic, naive people determined to "save" the civilian population by transforming them into Americans. When Hanks' character is sent to a small native hamlet, he clashes with the well-meaning Beth Wexler (played by Rita Wilson) as the two join forces to save the residents from a brutal warlord. Eventually realizing his responsibility to his fellow humans, Hanks' reluctant hero reveals his compassionate side and earns Beth's love.

Hanks' most recent film job allowed him to play a multidimensional character who is both a glib, cynical aristocrat and a budding hero. Hanks acknowledged that his Volunteers role was "the first job I've had where gut instinct was not all that was necessary." The actor studied with a speech coach to perfect his diction for the role of the urbane playboy. Furthermore, Hanks, who is a casual—almost sloppy—dresser in real life, was advised by the film's costume designer on his premium outfit.

Despite his reservations about playing the Volunteers, Hanks performed admirably during filming. Later, the film's director, Nicholas Meyer, stated, "He was always very professional; there was nothing you could fault; he would do anything you'd ask him, but he wasn't prepared to reveal himself as a human being." While Hanks maintained an invisible emotional bubble around most of the cast, he let down his guard with his leading lady. He discovered he had a fantastic rapport with Wilson, who was 26 at the time. Wilson was born Margarita Ibrahimoff in Los Angeles, the daughter of a Greek mother and a Bulgarian father.

Rita had been modeling since she was a child. Later, she worked in TV advertisements and spent a year studying acting at London's Academy of Music and Dramatic Art. Before getting cast in Volunteers, she had appeared in a couple TV movies and feature films. In reality, she had appeared as a guest star on an episode of Hanks' sitcom Bosom Buddies in 1981, albeit she and Hanks shared minimal on-screen time during that section. Now in Mexico filming Volunteers, Hanks describes Wilson as "amazingly cool, not cocky." On and off the set, the two spent a lot of time together. However, their connection remained platonic because Hanks was still unhappily married to Samantha and was involved with someone back in Los Angeles.

Volunteers debuted in August 1985. According to critics, the picture featured an awkward mix of slapstick comedy, satire, idealism, romance, and drama. Nonetheless, Hanks received positive feedback, including from Newsweek's David Ansen, who stated that "his character requires both the outside smirk of a Bill Murray and the debonair inside moves of a Cary Grant, and Hanks has both."

FIGHTING AN UPHILL BATTLE

The Money Pit (1985), a remake of Cary Grant's 1948 comedic blockbuster Mr. Blandings Builds His Dream House, found Hanks in full Cary Grant mode. In this wide farce, Hanks and his screen wife (Cheers' Shelley Long) are two New Yorkers who go to the country. They rapidly learn that their large new home requires a large number of costly and time-consuming repairs. The couple's marriage is on the verge of disintegration as they deal with different renovation disasters. By this point, Hollywood had established that no matter what sort or level of picture Hanks performed in, he was an extraordinarily appealing actor to whom viewers responded enthusiastically. Despite multiple aesthetic missteps, Hanks' asking cost per film continued to rise. He made $750,000 per episode of The Money Pit. And he deserved it.

Hanks' film performance required considerable physical agility as he performed pratfalls, was plastered, and ducked an incredible array of flying debris on the construction-site scene. To make matters worse, such difficult moments frequently had to be replayed numerous times in order to get all of the necessary aspects on film. Despite the physical toll of such stunts, Hanks' adventurous inner kid rose to the role's tough challenges. "From my perspective, there's an element of danger that you don't find in most professions." I enjoy being the only person on the set who does not wear a protective face cover during the shoot."

The Money Pit, which cost $10 million to make, made $37.5 million in domestic distribution. It is not a film that most moviegoers remember fondly because of too many predictable sight gags. Nothing in Common (1986), Hanks' next picture, was chosen for a variety of reasons. For starters, it provided him with the opportunity to work alongside Jackie Gleason, the renowned stage, TV, and film comic who had previously proved his excellent acting ability in films such as The Hustler (1961). For another, Hanks would reunite with veteran director and producer Garry Marshall, who had previously directed Hanks' Happy Days TV debut a few years before. Finally, this new project gave the budding star the opportunity to combine comedy and drama on camera. Hanks believed he was now prepared to take on a challenging task that required him to "tone it down, rein it in, and start trying to tell the truth, as opposed to just telling a joke."

Even more important to Hanks than his spectacular $1 million pay for the film (part of a three-movie development deal with Columbia Pictures) was the fact that he felt personally committed to the film's plot. Nothing in Common follows the divorce of a long-married couple (Gleason and Eva Marie Saint). Following that, Gleason loses his job and finds himself in the hospital with severe diabetic complications. This succession of family problems causes Hanks' character, the couple's brash advertising executive son, to rethink his detached approach to life and to truly know and respect his parents in their time of need. These plot lines paralleled Hanks' real-life relationship with his father, Amos, who had suffered from serious kidney problems for many years and had nearly died on multiple occasions. Amos had two kidney transplants in the 1980s, but his health remained perilous. After years of merely passing communication, the ongoing circumstance pushed father and son much closer together.

Nothing in Common's awkward blend of comedy and drama perplexed audiences, and the movie performed only reasonably well at the box office. Nonetheless, Hanks was pleased with the project, which displayed his versatility as an actor. A reviewer for the Los Angeles Times praised Hanks for his ability to "sustain beautifully a growing seriousness."

BOX OFFICE FODDER

Meanwhile, another of Hanks' films, Every Time We Say Goodbye, was released briefly in 1986. It was a love story set in Jerusalem during World War II between an American pilot and a young Jewish woman. The ill-conceived Tristar film was only shown in a few cinemas in the United States.

Much more well-known was Hanks' appearance in Dragnet (1987), an elaborate film pastiche of the legendary TV police series that aired in the 1950s and 1960s. Hanks opted to play a supporting role in the Universal production in order to collaborate with Dan Aykroyd. He played Aykroyd's unconventional Los Angeles Police Department partner. Hanks had to tone down his comic act as a clumsy, trouble-prone undercover detective since Dan portrayed his role incredibly deadpan. Unfortunately, many critics and spectators found Hanks' character to be dull and one-dimensional, as did the majority of the picture. As a result, the costly film performed miserably.

Hanks has played a prominent role in eight films in a relatively short period of time, several of them were commercial and/or artistic flops. He began to worry if both his marriage and his profession were doomed.

CHAPTER 5
HITTING THE BIG TIME

Only a few people close to Tom Hanks were aware that he had moved out of his North Hollywood house in 1985. His marital issues with Samantha had worsened as his acting career progressed, and she was depressed in her role as a housewife. Hanks' constant departure from home while filming fostered the increasing schism between him and Samantha.

Hanks felt the most awful about spending so little time with his two young children. For Hanks, parenting had passed in a whirlwind, with the majority of his time spent away on filming locations. Hanks attempted to mend his marriage by assisting his wife in reactivating her acting career, assisting her when she produced and acted in a theatrical performance. Their marital problems, though, appeared to be beyond resolve. As their position deteriorated, the couple realized that divorce was their only option. After reaching that conclusion, Hanks realized something disturbing: "Oh my God; my kids are going to feel as lonely as I did [as a child]."

While Hanks and Samantha were going through the difficult divorce procedures, he and Rita Wilson began dating and attending industry gatherings together.

Hanks and Samantha separated in 1987 after months of acrimonious fighting over custody of their two children, who went to Samantha, and a financial distribution of their possessions. To avoid his children feeling abandoned, Hanks made every effort to stay involved in their lives, frequently taking them on site for his current film and attending major milestones in their lives.

Regarding his relationship with his ex-wife, Hanks subsequently stated, "Their mother and I don't talk much anymore, but we're very respectful of each other." I wouldn't call us pals, much less friendly. But we are very respectful of one other's status and situation." Samantha and her two children moved to northern California after their divorce.

On New Year's Eve 1987, Hanks proposed to Rita Wilson. Her response was a triumphant "You bet!" To impress Rita, Hanks joined the Greek Orthodox Church. The pair married on April 30, 1988, in a large ceremony attended by relatives and friends in Los Angeles. The couple spent their honeymoon in the Caribbean.

BIG CHANGES

Even during this period of significant transition in his personal life, Hanks maintained his rigorous filmmaking schedule. When Harrison Ford, Warren Beatty, and finally Robert De Niro all dropped out of the lead part in Big (1988), director Penny Marshall (the sister of filmmaker Garry Marshall) went to her friend Tom Hanks. She asked him to star in this screen comedy co-written by Anne Spielberg, Steven Spielberg's sister. Hanks swiftly accepted the $1.75 million role. "What I dug about it was there were no car chases, no bad guys, no guns," Hanks said of the production. "A large portion of the film is just two people sitting around talking."

Big is the story of a 12-year-old child who wishes to become an adult. The next morning, he awakens to discover that he is now 35 years old, and no one believes his explanation for the sudden transformation. Later, he finds a job with a huge toy business and quickly rises to the rank of executive. He meets a lovely employee (Elizabeth Perkins) at the firm. She instantly falls in love with him after being won over by his youthful charm. Toward the end of the film, the hero realizes he misses being a teenager and uses the wish-granting machine to convert himself back into a child.

Big Hanks acknowledged his inner child—and it paid off. To play the youngster properly, the actress had to go through a difficult process: "It required a lot of paring back of stuff I'd done before, and done with some success." This is not a particularly talkative or confrontational man. I've played vocal, aggressive, sarcastic, and caustic characters. I have to play someone who was literally innocent in this case." Although Hanks became frustrated with Penny Marshall's propensity of continuously practicing situations, he learned that the practice was tremendously beneficial. The method instilled immense confidence in the actor's grasp of a scene, allowing him to improvise imaginatively within the parameters of his character.

In June 1988, it was released. Big received numerous media endorsements. Time magazine's Gerald Clark praised the picture, writing, "Hanks, who emerges from this film as one of Hollywood's top comic actors, is both believable and touching as a boy lost in a grown-up world." According to Janet Maslin of the New York Times, "Mr. Hanks is an absolute delight." Big generated $115 million in domestic distribution despite costing $18 million to produce. Hanks was nominated for an Academy Award for Best Actor for his performance, which he lost to Dustin Hoffman for his portrayal in Rain Man.

Punchline (1988), a film made before but released after Big, is about a housewife and mother (Sally Field) who aspires to be a stand-up comic. At an amateur night competition, she meets Steven Gold (Hanks), a smart, acerbic, emerging comedian. She soon begins to rely on him for career advice, and the two develop love feelings for one another. The couple battle for a chance to participate on a prominent TV show in a televised competition. By that point, Field's character must decide whether to stay with her husband or go with Hanks' character, a sad guy tortured by emotional problems from his past.

Hanks faced two huge artistic obstacles in Punchline: first, he had to portray a fairly unpleasant character, and second, he had to execute actual stand-up comedy routines. Hanks was especially worried about doing stand-up comedy, something he had previously avoided because he felt it was above his skills. He recognized, however, that confronting this creative risk would make him a stronger all-around performer. The film's writer and director, David Seltzer, encouraged Hanks to perform in actual comedy clubs and develop his own stand-up material. The resulting practice could be used in the film, providing the actor with insights on his characterization. "Eventually, after the entire course of shooting [Punchline], I had a 40-minute act," Hanks remarked of the arduous process. We had a genuine stand-up comedy performance that was hilarious in and of itself. As a result, it was more of a preparatory activity than research. This was a once-in-a-lifetime opportunity."

Despite the fact that it was released in September 1988, after Big's triumph, Punchline did not receive the critical accolades that Hanks had in Big. Many critics thought Punchline was an uncomfortable blend of comedy and drama, with underdeveloped love undertones. Punchline, which cost $15 million to make, barely made $21 million in domestic distribution. Despite the lackluster response from the public and critics, Hanks has no regrets about producing this entry. "It's the best work I've ever done," Hanks commented in 1989. We were discussing some very raw realities about the characters and, in many ways, about myself." These truths included Hanks' own incapacity to properly balance his professional and personal life, as well as temper his very competitive character.

STUCK IN A CAREER RUT

Hanks was in high demand after the success of Big, and he was receiving huge picture proposals on a regular basis. Among the scripts he received, Hanks turned down lead roles in critically acclaimed films such as Dead Poets Society and Field of Dreams. Instead, he created The 'burbs, a bizarre satire of suburban life. The narrative, which stars Carrie Fisher as his wife and Bruce Dern as one of his peculiar neighbors, revolves around suburbanites exploring the eerie home of a strange family who has relocated into their close-knit neighborhood. The film was a black comedy that was half social satire, part horror spoof, but it never effectively focused on either genre. Even Tom Hanks, Hollywood's most endearing newcomer, was chastised for his portrayal of a house owner on the verge of a nervous breakdown. "Hanks throws himself into this anti-audience movie with such suave energy that he seems determined to torpedo his hard-won reputation as Hollywood's most comfortable new star," wrote Richard Corliss for Time.

Hanks next appeared in Turner & Hooch (1989), as part of a new deal with Disney. It was a buddy comedy in which he was paired with one of the ugliest dogs in film. Before filming began, Hanks spent a significant amount of time bonding with his canine co-star.

While it was not one of Hanks's more difficult tasks, nor is it one of his favorites, Turner & Hooch did pretty well at the box office, grossing $71.1 million in domestic distribution. The film's director, Roger Spottiswoode, remarked of Hanks' dedication during production, "I never worked with an actor who is as much a film-maker and who takes a great deal of responsibility for the film without being an interferer."
In 1989, Hanks returned to Saturday Night Live (which he had previously hosted) to take part in the variety show 15th anniversary special.

AN OFFBEAT ENTRY

Next In Joe Versus the Volcano (1990), an offbeat romantic comedy produced by Steven Spielberg's Amblin Entertainment, Hanks played a hypochondriac. Hanks as Joe, a modest clerk with a slew of fictitious afflictions. After being diagnosed with a deadly disease, Hanks' character accepted an extraordinary offer from an eccentric billionaire: enjoy his remaining time in opulent luxury in exchange for performing a human sacrifice to a volcano on a Polynesian island at the conclusion of this period. Meg Ryan portrayed Hanks' coworker as well as the strange entrepreneur's two daughters.

From the beginning, Hanks recognized that this one-of-a-kind screen fable may turn off spectators unless all of the pieces came together right. Despite this, he agreed to feature in the hazardous film for a $3.5 million salary because "I liked the emotional journey that Joe Banks [the lead character] was on." Joe Versus the Volcano was a huge flop when it was released, with much of the responsibility falling on first-time director John Patrick Shanley (who also created the script).

The Bonfire Of The Vanities And Radio Flyer

If Joe Versus the Volcano was a flop, it paled in contrast to The Bonfire of the Vanities. This project was inspired by Tom Wolfe's best-selling novel of the same name, which was published in 1987 and is a stinging satire about race and class in 1980s New York City. The plot revolves around a snooty, self-indulgent Wall Street financier. When he and his mistress hit an African-American youngster with their car in a tough south Bronx area, his selfish life falls apart. The cops track down and arrest the rich man's vehicle's owner. The sensationalized trial that follows brings together a diverse array of special interest organizations to advocate for a conviction.

Warner Bros. had won the Hollywood bidding war for The Bonfire of the Vanities' film rights. Then came a succession of bizarre judgments involving crucial film assignments. Surprisingly, Brian De Palma, known for his thrillers, was chosen to direct the big-budget play. Because the book had been so well-received, there was a lot of speculation about who might portray the important characters. Sterling actor William Hurt was a major contender for the role of Sherman McCoy, but De Palma insisted on Hanks. "I think Tom Hanks is the best comedic actor around who can convey a serious side," the director reasoned. And there's no doubt in my opinion that playing drama is simpler than playing comic timing."

When he was first approached for the high-profile part, Hanks was concerned that he was not the right person for the role. Many in his immediate circle shared his first reaction to the job offer. However, because this was such a significant opportunity, Hanks was humbled to be invited to be a part of it. "I wasn't about to say, 'Well, gee, I can't do the role.'" Hanks agreed to do the role for a $5 million salary.

Several cast decisions in The Bonfire of the Vanities were perplexing. Melanie Griffith, known for her attractiveness rather than her acting ability, was cast in the tough role of Hanks' birdbrained sweetheart. Bruce Willis, the smirky star of the action film Die Hard (1988), was cast as a disillusioned, drunken journalist who rebuilds his career by reporting on the big trial. The choice of actor to play the film's spirited Jewish judge was perhaps the biggest surprise of all. De Palma chose well-known African-American actor Morgan Freeman for the role after unsuccessful bids for Walter Matthau and Alan Arkin. To accommodate the change in the judge's ethnicity, the plot of the film had to be rewritten.

Hanks spent time on Wall Street researching this key position, visiting with bond dealers to see what made them tick. The actress was awed by the sheer grandeur of the complex production as filming began in several sections of New York City. It made Hanks question if the film would come together effectively.

The Bonfire of the Vanities, which was released over the 1990 Christmas season, was hardly a festive pleasure. The film cost $47 million to make but only grossed $15.7 million in American distribution. It quickly became known as Hollywood's worst turkey in recent years.

In the aftermath of this box-office flop, the press constantly asked Hanks if he was unaware that something was wrong during the shoot. "It feels the same whether you're filming a hit or a flop," he said. Following the negative public reaction to the film, Hanks attempted to forget about The Bonfire of the Vanities. However, given all of the negative press, this was a challenging task. The birth of Hanks and Rita's son Chester in 1990 offset this career setback.

Radio Flyer, shot in the fall of 1990 but not released until early 1992, rounded out Hanks' run of professional disappointments. The unusual story was a tough blend of fantasy and child abuse issues. Hanks, who elected not to be listed in the film's credits, narrates the story and appears briefly at the film's beginning and end. In the film, he tells his young sons about the unusual happenings he and his brother witnessed throughout their turbulent upbringing. The flawed film was likewise commercially unsuccessful.

At this point, Hanks took a step back to reconsider his film career. Hanks recognized that too many of his 14 films during the previous six years did not meet his personal standards. It caused him to step away from filmmaking for a while in order to reconsider his previous strategy of selecting films in which he wished to appear. He understood that his approach to acting had been wrong up to this point: "It became a matter of just getting it done, as opposed to doing it right," he remarked. With his life suddenly free of professional constraints, he spent a lot of time with his family, went surfing and skiing, and did everything he could to aid his father during Amos' dying years.

Hanks overhauled talent management as he cleaned his mind and reconsidered his profession. At the same time, he met with his good friend Penny Marshall to see if she would consider casting him in her new film, A League of Their Own (1992).

CHAPTER 6
LIFE IS LIKE A BOX OF CHOCOLATES

"It was the best thing for everybody," Tom Hanks stated of his nearly 19-month hiatus from filmmaking. I needed to get away from the industry. And the industry needs a break from me for a time."

When Hanks returned to acting, he was determined to pursue only roles that were both demanding for him and relevant to audiences. He told his new talent agency, the powerful Creative Artists, that he wanted to play tougher, more mature characters than he had in the past, characters that would complement his age and acting expertise.

A LEAGUE OF THEIR OWN

Prior to his hiatus from filmmaking, Hanks was approached about a role in A League of Their Own (1992), a baseball narrative with a twist. The video focused on the little-remembered women's professional teams that emerged during World War II, when the majority of the male players were participating in the war. Hanks initially turned down the job of manager because it was not a starring role. He now went hat in hand to Penny Marshall, who had just been hired on to direct the period comedy. She was skeptical of her friend's pick for the role of Jimmy Dugan, an overweight, alcoholic former baseball player who coaches the all-girls baseball team, because of Hanks' recent record of high-profile disasters and since he normally played the leading man in movies. Hanks stated that he was willing to go to any length to bring Dugan's repulsive demeanor to life. Marshall eventually gave in.

Hanks put on 30 pounds for the job. He also proposed that his middle-aged character walk with a limp (from an old sports injury) so that people don't question why the coach remained a civilian during WWII. While Hanks was preparing for the role, Marshall recruited an intriguing cast of baseball players, including Geena Davis, Madonna, and Rosie O'Donnell.

A League of Their Own, which was shot on location in Evansville, Indiana, was released in midsummer 1992. The $40 million film was a great hit with audiences, generating $107 million in domestic distribution. Among the accolades for the picture, Hanks received his fair share. The New York Times' Vincent Canby concluded, "With his work here, there can be no doubt that Mr. Hanks is now one of Hollywood's most accomplished and self-assured actors."

Hanks' gamble with A League of Their Own has reaped huge rewards. He not only proved he had a considerably broader acting range than Hollywood insiders had anticipated, but he also had a lot of fun in the quirky part. "The whole reason I did this movie was because it was going to be a blast," he laughed. Play baseball with a lot of females all summer? Please! Please assist me. And be compensated for it? Fine. I'll be there. "When do we begin?"

SLEEPLESS IN SEATTLE

Hanks saw A League of Their Own as the beginning of his "modern era" of filmmaking, in which he focused on more genuine, dimensional roles. With this in mind, he re-joined forces with Meg Ryan for Sleepless in Seattle (1993). This romantic love story would propel the actor from a famous leading man to a great Hollywood celebrity.

Sleepless in Seattle, directed by Nora Ephron (who also wrote the screenplay), was a glossy tearjerker that owes a lot to An Affair to Remember (1957), which featured Cary Grant and Deborah Kerr. Hanks plays a recent Seattle widower who, through a series of unlikely and humorous occurrences, finds love in New York City with a lady he barely knows (Meg Ryan) and never meets in person until the film's conclusion. Despite the fact that Ryan and Hanks had limited actual screen time in Sleepless in Seattle, Meg was excited to work with Hanks again. "He can find so much in such a short period of time.... His work is straightforward, and he always finds the strongest way to convey the most. Something about him makes you feel like you can just fill in the blanks."

Sleepless in Seattle grossed $127 million at the domestic box office. Hanks' Cary Grant-like performance was credited with much of the film's popularity. "The best reason to see [Sleepless] is Tom Hanks," one critic said, "but then he's always the best reason to see a movie."

Not only was Hank's back on top in Hollywood, but he was also branching out into other areas of show business. He began directing episodes of TV shows, such as Fallen Angels, Tales from the Crypt, and a teleseries adaptation of A League of Their Own. These assignments influenced Hanks' desire to direct his own feature film.

PHILADELPHIA

After British actor Daniel Day-Lewis was unable to appear in Philadelphia (1993), director Jonathan Demme cast Tom Hanks in the controversial main role in this AIDS thriller. Demme stated that one of the key reasons he chose Hanks was because "as a personality, Tom had the trust and confidence of Americans, which I felt would help us reach across to a mainstream audience." When Hanks agreed to take the job, he was aware that he was taking a significant career risk. He would play Andrew Beckett, a successful attorney who gets sacked from his respected Pennsylvania law practice once his AIDS is found. There was a fear in Hollywood at the time—and still is—that portraying a gay on-screen character would "tarnish" an actor's macho image and jeopardize his potential to be cast as a heterosexual leading man in the future.

Hanks defied those counsel who advised him to decline Philadelphia. He reasoned that his odd childhood, full of unexpected relocations and rapidly shifting family groups, had taught him what it felt like to be an outsider. "I felt from the very beginning that I had an awful lot in common with the character of Andrew Beckett [in Philadelphia]," the actor told CNN's Larry King. I thought he was similar to me in many elements of my background and my current outlook on life. The fact that he was a gay man with a fatal disease was, you know, in there, but I didn't see it as a major impediment."

To prepare for this difficult job, Hanks spoke with medical experts on the realities of AIDS. He also met with AIDS patients who described their sufferings, worries, and discrimination as a result of the condition. Hanks learnt a lot about the condition and how it affects people's life on many levels during this grueling research process. Hanks recalled meeting an AIDS patient who "told me that when he was first diagnosed, he went to the window and thought, 'Clouds, this is the last time I am going to see you.'" "I was thinking about that when I was doing a scene in the film, and it brought tears to my eyes."

Hanks shed 30 pounds and had his hair increasingly chopped down throughout filming to establish visual credibility as an AIDS patient. This, combined with sophisticated cosmetics, enabled him to achieve the gaunt appearance of a dying man. "I'm not a big method actor," Hanks admitted. I don't completely immerse myself in a character. But I am touched by everything I do, and I found myself on this one crying at the most fantastic and ridiculous things."

Philadelphia was just as contentious when it was released. Many homosexual activist organizations felt that Hanks and his on-screen partner should have had more intimate moments in the film. Other groups complained that the plot's homosexual characters were too stereotypical. Despite these criticisms, Philadelphia, which cost $26 million to make, grossed $201 million worldwide and affected viewers all around the world. According to the New York Times, "in the end, thanks to... the simple grace of Mr. Hanks's performance, this film does accomplish what it set out to do." Philadelphia rises above its faults to portray and drive home the entire seriousness of its challenging topic."

On March 21, 1994, a proud but befuddled Tom Hanks walked onto the platform of Los Angeles' Dorothy Chandler Pavilion to accept the Academy Award for Best Actor for his performance in Philadelphia. "My work is magnified by the fact that the streets of heaven are too crowded with angels—we know their names," Hanks said before launching into a lengthy monologue. They number in the thousands for each of the red ribbons [red lapel buttons symbolizing AIDS awareness] that we are wearing here tonight."

PICKING ANOTHER WINNER

After his victory in Philadelphia, Hanks had little time to relax and enjoy his personal life, which now included residences in Los Angeles, Malibu, and New York City. He'd already discovered a new picture that had piqued his interest: Forrest Gump (1994), based on Winston Groom's 1986 novel of the same name. The plot is around a simple yet remarkable man with a low IQ who embarks on a series of extraordinary adventures over the course of several years, including meetings with several U.S. presidents and other world leaders.

This outlandish fable was deemed dangerous since its main character was so unlike the typical Hollywood movie character. However, Hanks believed the picture and its simple, plain principal character were refreshing. Hanks admired the role for "the purity of how he sees the world." "All the great stories are about our battle against loneliness," he said when he agreed to star in the film. That's what I've always been drawn to." Rather than accepting a flat payment, Hanks agreed to take a part of the film's profits. As a result of his risk, the celebrity earned an estimated $60 million for this film.

Forrest Gump, directed by Robert Zemeckis and released by Paramount in the summer of 1994, was a huge success. It achieved a $674 million global profit on a $55 million investment. Much of the film's acclaim went to Hanks, who played the humble Gump and delivered memorable lines like "Mama always said life was like a box of chocolates." You never know what you'll get."

The Forrest Gump sensation was so huge, inspiring extensive merchandising tie-ins, that Hollywood experts worried that an aversion to the film's tremendous success might hurt the film's chances in the following Oscar race. On the contrary, the film received 13 Academy win nominations and won six, including Hanks' second consecutive Best Actor win. A beaming Hanks honored his wife, Rita, at the ceremony, saying she "has taught me and demonstrates to me every day just what love is."

With the public's enthusiastic support for Forrest Gump, Hanks had become one of the film industry's most powerful characters.

HEADING TO OUTER SPACE

Hanks had been interested in America's space program since he was a child. When Hanks learned that his old buddy Ron Howard was working on the film Apollo 13 (1995), he was eager to get involved and fulfill his childhood dream of dressing up in astronaut garb. He enthusiastically informed Howard that he would portray any crewmember in the script. Howard cast two-time Oscar winner Tom Hanks as Jim Lovell, a critical astronaut aboard the spacecraft's abortive lunar mission in 1970.

To prepare for this important part, Hanks spent time on the ground and in the air (in a small plane) with the actual Jim Lovell, a heroic man who, according to Hanks, "went through an almost superhuman experience." Hanks also spent a significant amount of time reviewing NASA transcripts of the actual Apollo 13 voyage as well as any accessible background information on the near-fatal space journey.

By the time production on Apollo 13 began, Hanks had become so well-prepared that Howard and his crew frequently used him as an informal technical counsel. Indeed, executive producer Brian Grazer stated, "Tom was at least 50% of the driving force behind this film." He was the movie's truth meter because of his grasp of what truly happened on that mission.... Tom helped police the film's tone by making it very obvious what it should be."

Despite the fact that the majority of Apollo 13 was shot on studio soundstages, Howard used an actual space simulator to produce the zero-gravity aircraft in which the characters would be seen contending with weightlessness during their perilous outer-space voyage. The attention to detail added to the reality of this stunning recreation of an American vessel.

The public reacted enthusiastically to this epic play. According to Variety, the film hit "a commercial bull's-eye." According to Time magazine, Hanks "provides the anchor." His Lovell—as strong, loyal, and emotionally honest as Forrest Gump—carries the story like a rare oxygen bag. Lovell gains power from his inventiveness, and the film gains empathy from his ability to portray fear." Hanks' contribution was worth the $17.5 million he was paid for his role in Apollo 13, which made $334 million worldwide.

NO TIME TO BREATHE

In 1995, Hanks took part in The Celluloid Closet, a documentary that traced the history of gay and lesbian characters and themes in American films. Hanks also gave the voice of Woody, the old-fashioned toy cowboy, in the computer-animated picture Toy Story that year. Truman Hanks, Hanks and Rita's second son, was born in 1995.

After directing TV episodes, Hanks achieved his desire to create a full film, That Thing You Do! (1996), in which he drew on his boyhood memories and passion for British pop groups' invasion of American music in the 1960s. The film follows a youthful group of small-town Pennsylvania musicians as they soar to the top of the charts as one-hit wonders in 1964. The plot then delves into how their sudden career change affects the group. Hanks wrote, produced, and directed the picture, as well as appearing in a small role and writing some of the songs. While That Thing You Do! was a moderate box office success, working 18-hour days and seeing so little of his family prompted Hanks to return to acting. This led to Hanks accepting an offer from longtime friend and Malibu Beach neighbor Steven Spielberg to star in Saving Private Ryan (1998), a big World War II epic.

CHAPTER 7
LIVING AT THE TOP

When creating Saving Private Ryan, his epic World War II film, director Steven Spielberg intended to break from the Hollywood habit of glamorizing battle on the big screen. He wanted to represent the misery of battle, where there were no true winners. Hanks agreed wholeheartedly with Spielberg's viewpoint. "It's difficult to understand the violence equation," Hanks told People magazine. That there are two sides to an equal sign--pull the trigger on a machine gun, make a loud glamorous noise, and it's a lot of fun; but on the other side of the equation, white-hot chunks of metal fly through people's skin, causing their heads to explode, and they die. Or they'll be maimed for life. [Audiences] do not add the two elements together."

Before beginning filming on Saving Private Ryan, Spielberg put his primary players undergo grueling boot camp training. A retired Marine commander was in charge of getting the actors in condition for the grueling location filming.

The film, set in 1944, follows a U.S. Army squad led by Hanks' character, a former schoolteacher. They are directed to travel into German-occupied France in order to rescue a soldier whose three brothers have already been killed in action; this soldier is to be sent home, sparing his family the loss of another son. Several squad members are slain by the enemy while accomplishing the perilous task. Hanks' character, an average man thrust into extraordinary circumstances, finds comedy in the reality that in order to save one person, others must perish. He is, nonetheless, obligated to carry out his Army commands.

The graphic opening 20 minutes of this extended film were a highlight for many viewers. This footage depicted the dreadful D-Day invasion on June 6, 1944, as Allied forces--including Hanks and his men--landed on enemy-held Omaha Beach in Normandy. The gore and bloodshed depicted in this horrible scenario remain unforgettable. This graphic portion, like the rest of this realistic documentary, depicts the valor of American soldiers battling till death for a cause in which they truly believed.

Saving Private Ryan was well received by critics, and Hanks was praised for his performance as the commander. According to the San Francisco Chronicle, "in an honest, foursquare performance, Hanks embodies the spirit of simple decency, one of the reasons for which the war was fought." "In Hanks's performance," the Chronicle reporter continued, "there is no doubt in my mind that he has taken the mantle of the quintessential American actor that once belonged to Jimmy Stewart."

Saving Private Ryan grossed $216 million in domestic distribution and another $227.4 million in international distribution for a budget of $70 million. The film got 11 Oscar nominations, including one for Best Actor for Tom Hanks. Despite having won two Academy Awards, Hanks was worried before the awards event. Despite losing the coveted Oscar to Italian actor Roberto Benigni, he was overjoyed that viewers had reacted so well to Spielberg's unglamorous picture of battle.

While filming Saving Private Ryan, Hanks became aware of a fundraising initiative in the United States to build a national memorial for World War II veterans. He believed so strongly in the initiative that he volunteered to appear in tapped public-service advertisements to bring the fund-raiser to the public's attention.

TALKING ON NEW CHALLENGES

It had been five years since Hanks had appeared in a comedy film. As a versatile performer, he reunited with Meg Ryan for the 1998 romantic comedy You've Got Mail. In the film, Hanks plays the successful owner of a bookshop chain who meets Ryan over email. She owns a neighborhood bookstore in Manhattan, which Hanks' company is threatening to close. In judging this extremely popular movie entry, the New York Times praised Hanks's "romantic wistfulness," "poignant shyness," and "lovely way of speaking from the heart."

During the production of his two 1998 films, Hanks also appeared in From the Earth to the Moon, a 12-part HBO-cable series on the Apollo space missions of the 1960s and 1970s. In addition to producing the film, Hanks wrote four of the pieces, acted in the miniseries, and directed the first episode. Hanks shared an Emmy Award for Outstanding Miniseries as one of the project's producers.

Following that, Hanks starred in The Green Mile (1999), a drama based on Stephen King's six-part work of fiction. Hanks plays the head guard on death row at a 1930s Louisiana penitentiary in the film. Hanks' character meets one of the guilty guys and realizes that he possesses miraculous healing powers. Hanks garnered numerous positive reviews for his performance in this amazing story. In 1999, Hanks returned to voice work for the part of Woody in Toy Story 2.

The American Museum of the Moving Image honored Hanks with a renowned homage in April 1999. More than 800 people gathered at the Waldorf-Astoria Hotel in New York City to honor Hanks, 42. He was the prize's youngest recipient, as he was in 2002 when he received the American Film Institute's Lifetime Achievement award.

INTO THE NEW MILLENNIUM

For Cast Away (2000), a film distributed by Twentieth Century-Fox and DreamWorks, Steven Spielberg's new film firm, Tom Hanks reunited with Forrest Gump director Robert Zemeckis. The picture, for which Hanks wrote the main plot and served as producer, provided interesting challenges for the now-superstar actor. The plot saw Hanks' character stuck alone on an isolated Pacific island for four years after his plane crashed. Rather than depending on makeup and special effects to illustrate the drastic differences between Hanks' character before and after the crash, it was agreed that Hanks and the team would return to Hollywood following the initial shoot in Fiji. Hanks went on a strict diet for several months, losing more than 40 pounds and growing a full beard. At that moment, the actor and team returned to Fiji to finish the film.

For the majority of Cast Away, Hanks is the solitary performer on screen, illustrating his rituals of gathering food and attempting to retain his sanity and spirit despite years of loneliness. The actor conveyed his feelings and reactions with gestures and looks in the majority of these episodes, which had not spoken. It takes a competent and well-liked actor to keep an audience's attention through these types of moments, which may get tedious and predictable, and Hanks did it admirably. His performance was lauded by critics, and the picture performed well at the box office. For his role in Cast Away, Hanks garnered his fifth Best Actor Oscar nomination, but he lost to actor Russell Crowe.

Band of Brothers (2001) took up some of Hanks' time away from the two-part Cast Away filming. This 10-episode, 600-minute HBO miniseries was based on historian Stephen E. Ambrose's 1993 best-seller on the 101st Airborne's Easy Company. From the D-Day landing to the chase of fleeing German forces, the miniseries follows the company's traumatic combat experiences.

Hanks and Steven Spielberg were among the executive producers of this ambitious television production, which was inspired by Saving Private Ryan. Hanks not only directed one episode of the miniseries, but he also wrote another and played a British commander in another. Colin Hanks, Tom Hanks' son, played a soldier in the eighth episode of the huge production. The ambitious initiative garnered six Emmy Awards, giving Hanks multiple Emmy victories in his various technical positions.

On a more somber note, Hanks' first wife, Samantha, was stricken with cancer in 2002. Despite the fact that they had gone through difficult times and had not kept in touch on a regular basis, when Hanks realized she was ill, he brought her to Los Angeles to speak with the greatest medical doctors. Her health deteriorated, and she died in March 2002.

NEW ACTING VISTAS

Hanks accepted his first bad-guy cinematic part in Road to Perdition (2002), always eager to broaden his acting range. The violent picture is set in 1931 in the Midwest. Hanks portrays a hitman for the local gang boss, who is played by Paul Newman. Following the murders of Hanks' wife and younger son, the film follows him and his remaining kid as they seek to flee to safety, but with tragic repercussions.

Road to Perdition received mixed reviews, with many commentators praising its skill above its overall entertainment value. Hanks' shift from his usual good-guy portrayal drew mixed reactions.
Hanks returned to playing characters on the good side of the law in Catch Me If You Can (2002), co-starring alongside Leonardo DiCaprio. Hanks reunited with director Steven Spielberg for this picture. The DreamWorks film is based on the biography of Frank Abagnale Jr., a 16-year-old con artist who travels the world impersonating in various professions and writes bogus checks. In the film, Hanks plays an FBI agent who relentlessly pursues DiCaprio's brash young criminal.

Hanks gave an excellent performance as the workaholic cop, but critics argued his stiff role had to compete for viewer attention with DiCaprio's chameleon-like portrayal as the criminal. The fast-paced Catch Me If You Can, which cost $52 million to make, generated $164.4 million in domestic distribution.

In 2002, Hanks and his wife Rita invested in the romantic comedy My Big Fat Greek Wedding, a movie adaptation of Nia Vardalos' stage musical that was produced for a modest cost of $5 million. The independent film was the year's surprise hit, grossing $241 million in American distribution.

In 2003, pre-production on numerous new projects with Tom Hanks began. They include Robert Zemeckis' fantasy film The Polar Express, Steven Spielberg's love drama The Terminal, a reworking of a famous British comedy The Ladykillers, and A Cold Case, a murder mystery.

CAREER CHANGES AND OTHER PROJECTS

Many things changed for Hanks in the 1990s: he moved from comic to serious, dramatic acting; many of the roles he accepted became personal passions and projects for him; and he became more active in developing and producing films rather than merely performing in them.

Hanks' success in films like Forrest Gump, Apollo 13, and Saving Private Ryan not only gained him critical acclaim, but also demonstrated to film studios that Hanks was a financial benefit to film productions. At the height of his fame in 1998, Hanks took the next step and asked his pal Gary Goetzman to join him in creating a production company. With the assistance of Goetzman, the executive producer of Philadelphia and an experienced lyricist, Hanks evolved from an actor to a trusted producer. Playtone collaborates with major film studios to produce big-budget productions like Mamma Mia! and Cast Away. Playtone's reputation for completing films smoothly and without drama or hassles has enabled Hanks and Gary cultivate successful partnerships in Hollywood, allowing them to expand Playtone's projects to television, short films, documentaries, and IMAX pictures.

Hanks chooses Playtone assignments in the same way he chooses acting roles: depending on his personal interests and the strength of the story. Playtone was involved in the critically acclaimed cable television miniseries Band of Brothers, The Pacific, John Adams, and 1776, all of which focused on military history. In an homage to Gary's hobbies, Playtone also produced Mamma Mia! and the documentary Neil Young: Heart of Gold. Hanks and Gary have developed Playtone as one of Hollywood's most successful production businesses.

Gaining more clout in Hollywood through Playtone has only aided Hanks' pursuit of his interests in history and space exploration. Aside from his roles in Band of Brothers, Apollo 13, and Saving Private Ryan, Hanks has supported efforts to honor those who have served in previous conflicts, as well as space programs. Hanks and close friend

Steven Spielberg have contributed to the creation of a World War II Memorial in Washington, D.C., and have assisted in the fundraising and development of projects for the World War II Museum in New Orleans. Hanks was inducted into the Army's Ranger Hall of Fame (the first actor to get such honors), received the Douglas S. Morrow Public Outreach Award, and NASA even dedicated an asteroid after him in recognition of his efforts and dedication to these causes.

Despite the fact that these new endeavors consume much of Hanks' time, he has not ceased acting. He appeared in the films The Da Vinci Code and Angels & Demons, and he voiced a car in the animated feature Cars. His association with Playtone allows him to be both a producer and an actor on film projects, which he has done successfully in Charlie Wilson's War (for which he received a Golden Globe nomination for Best Actor), Larry Crowne, and The Great Buck Howard, a film starring his son, Colin. He has also narrated short films and documentaries, and he played Woody again in Toy Story 3. Hanks' film Extremely Loud and Incredibly Close was released in 2011, the same year he became a grandfather, and he appeared in the science fiction picture Cloud Atlas in 2012.

Hanks has spoken about slowing down, despite having numerous big-budget films and the industry's highest accolades on his record, but he has not ceased pushing himself to perfect his art. He made his Broadway debut in Nora Ephron's Lucky Guy in 2013, and was nominated for a Tony Award for his performance. Hanks featured in Captain Phillips the same year. Hanks and the film crew had to spend two months on freighters and military ships out in the ocean while playing a ship captain kidnapped by Somali pirates. Surviving the climate, on the other hand, was worthwhile: Hanks' performance as Captain Phillips received international acclaim. "As good as Hanks has been in the past," critic Kenneth Turan says in an L.A. Times film review, "there are moments here, especially near the conclusion, that are deeper and more emotional than anything we've seen from this actor before." Hanks would close the year with additional accolades for his performance as Walt Disney in the film Saving Mr. Banks.

LOOKING AHEAD

Tom Hanks' career has not slowed down. Hanks is a professional actor, producer, director, and writer who is beloved by fans all over the world. And he remains in high demand in Hollywood.

Hanks closed his victory speech at an awards ceremony in his honor a few years ago, "If I'm lucky, I'll have the chance to surprise you [moviegoers] some more." Given his perpetually packed filmmaking schedule, this guarantee seemed likely. After becoming a movie star as the screen's beloved everyman, Hanks appears to be most at ease these days playing a range of unselfish cinematic roles. He describes the issue of choosing screen segments as "finding things you haven't done before." There is no joy or future in doing the same thing again and over." Above all, he still considers his job to be one that "provides a great deal of joy." If you can obtain it, it's hard work, but it's also great work."

Hanks has learnt to better manage his frenetic job with his personal life and health in recent years, as he is now a grandfather and suffers from type 2 diabetes, which he announced in 2013. "At the end of the day," he says, "you have to tell yourself, 'Well, it's the end of the day.'" So you drive home to your family, eat a wonderful supper, and watch a darts tournament on TV. Some performers commit suicide by flog. I don't treat my profession like it's a carnival show. You are not required to work around the clock." In terms of his easygoing approach to daily life, the soft-spoken, unassuming, and relatively unflappable actor adds, "I probably have most of the worries everyone else does, but I just try not to worry too much."

Printed in Great Britain
by Amazon